Let's Talk

For AMY EHRLICH, who said YES!
With respect and affection – R. H. H. and M. E.

A NOTE TO PARENTS, TEACHERS, LIBRARIANS, CARERS,
HEALTH PROFESSIONALS, CLERGY AND ALL THOSE WHO SPEND
TIME WITH, CARE FOR OR WORK WITH YOUNG CHILDREN

Our young children are curious about almost everything. They are especially curious about their bodies, about where they came from, and how they were made. Many, but not all, ask us endless questions about these topics. They ask us why their bodies are the same and different from other people's bodies, what makes a girl a girl and a boy a boy, what the names are of all the different parts of their bodies, where babies come from, how babies are made, what a family is – and so many other questions about themselves and their bodies. Many of their questions are easy to answer. Others are more difficult to answer.

We created this book to answer young children's many questions and concerns about these issues. We talked with parents, teachers, librarians, nurses, doctors, social workers, psychologists, scientists, health professionals and clergy to make sure that all the material in this book is age-appropriate, scientifically accurate and, at this time, as up-to-date as possible. Many have asked us how best to use this book with children. There is no one answer. This book can be used as a shared experience between a child and an adult. Some children may want the book read to them from cover to cover. Other children may pick only the part or parts that interest them or answer a specific question they may have. And others may wish to look through or read the book on their own.

No matter which way our book is used, it is our hope that it will help answer young children's perfectly normal and amazing questions about their bodies, about where they came from and about what makes them either a boy or a girl.

Robie H. Harris and Michael Emberley, January 2006

Let's Talk

about Girls, Boys, Babies, Bodies, Families and Friends

Robie H. Harris   illustrated by Michael Emberley

WALKER BOOKS
AND SUBSIDIARIES
LONDON · BOSTON · SYDNEY · AUCKLAND

I can't WAIT to find out about ALL this stuff!

Contents

I CAN wait...

Let's go to the zoo and see the hippos!

I can't WAIT to go and see the insects!

Bird and Bee Go to the Zoo

1
So-ooo Many Questions!

You've probably seen all kinds of families – your own family, or a cousin's, friend's or neighbour's family – or a dog, cat, penguin, pig, hippo, horse, dolphin or elephant family – cuddling, loving, feeding, caring for and playing with their babies.

You may have lots of questions about where all these babies come from – and where you came from – and how you were made – and how you were born.

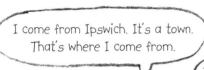

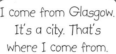

You may also wonder about what makes a baby a girl or a boy – and how girls and boys are the same and how they are different.

Asking questions is a great way to find out about lots of things. Asking a grown-up – your mummy, your daddy, or your aunt, uncle or grandparent, or a nurse or doctor – is a great way to find answers to your questions.

Looking through a book on your own, or asking your teacher or librarian or someone you know well to read a book to you, are other great ways to find answers.

11

Girls Do This, Boys Do That

Girls and boys – even baby girls and boys – are very different, you know!

Boys and girls – even baby boys and girls – are very the same, you know!

Girls catch fish and worms and creepy-crawlies!

So do boys!

Boys have very big and very strong muscles.

So do girls!

Girls play with dolls and teddy bears!

So do boys!

Boys play with trains, planes and trucks!

So do girls!

Girls sing and dance!

So do boys!

12

Same? Different?

One of the ways that you can tell boys and girls apart is by their bodies. Girls' and boys' bodies are mostly – but not exactly – the same.

Girls and women have a vagina. Boys and men have a penis. These are some of the special parts of our bodies that make us a boy or a man – or a girl or a woman.

Some of these parts are on the OUTSIDE of our bodies. They are the parts that are usually covered by pants, or a swimsuit, or – for babies and little kids – a nappy.

Some of these parts are INSIDE our bodies. But we cannot see the INSIDE parts with our own eyes.

I have 1 head, 2 wings, 1 body and 2 feet.

That's NOT a lot of parts!

Another thing that's different about boys and men and girls and women is how they use the loo. That's because some parts of their bodies are different. Pee comes out through a small opening at the tip of boys' and men's penises. Pee comes out through a small opening between girls' and women's legs.

That's why girls and women sit on the loo when they pee and why boys and men usually stand up when they pee. One thing that is the same for boys and men and girls and women is that they *all* sit on the loo when they poo.

Pee! Poo!
I love saying those words. They make me giggle.

That's silly! Everybody pees and poos!

One more thing that's different is that baby girls, girls and women are called "females" and baby boys, boys and men are called "males".

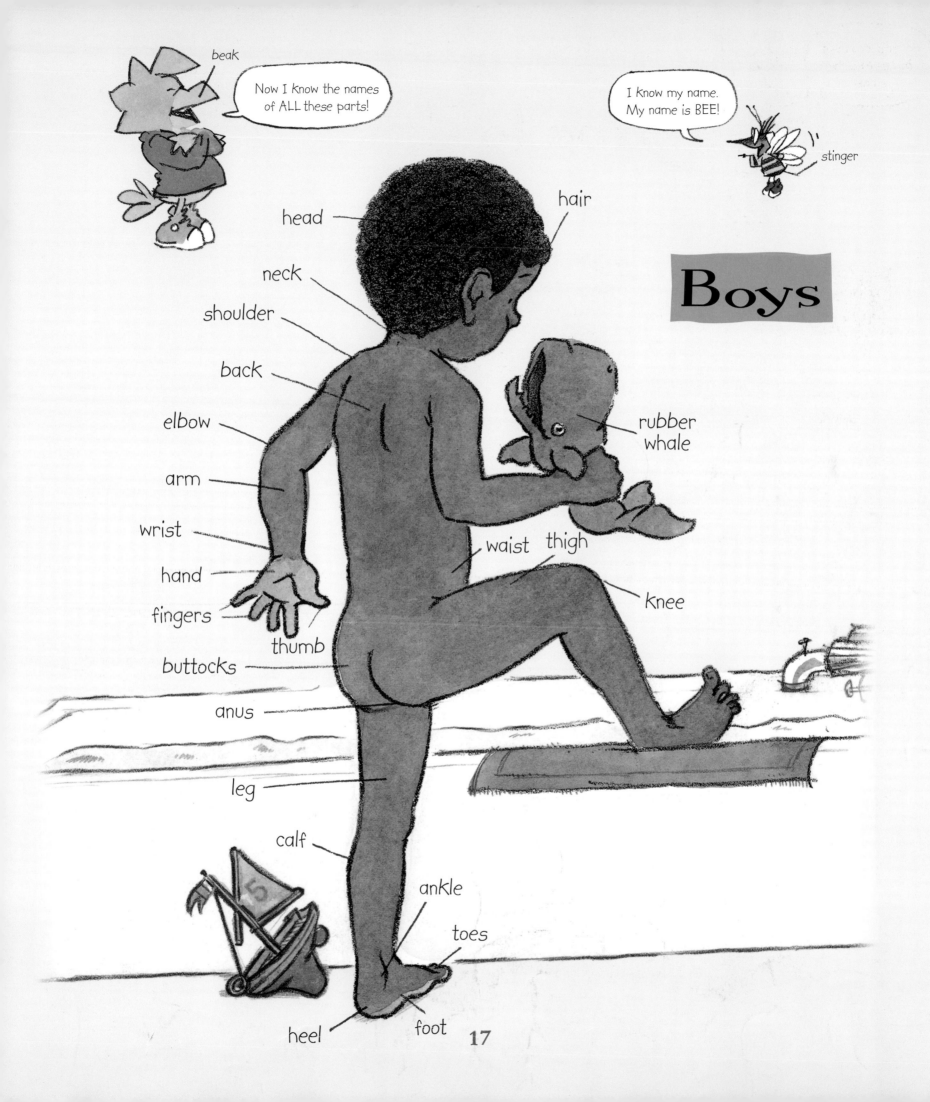

Head to Toe

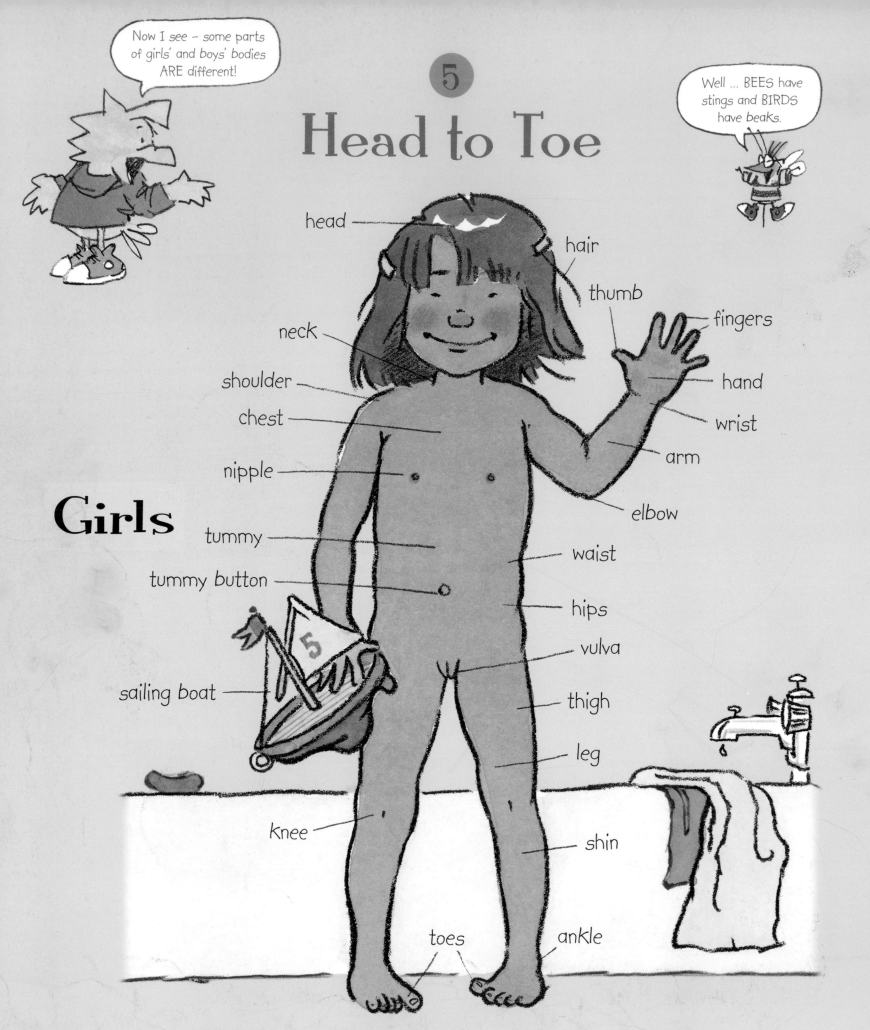

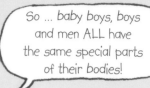

So ... ALL bees and birds have legs!

6
What Boys Have

Baby boys are born with special parts of their bodies – outside and inside – that make them boys.

The special OUTSIDE parts – the penis and the scrotum – hang between boys' and men's legs. That's why they are easy to see. Girls and women do not have these parts.

Two other OUTSIDE parts – the opening to the urethra and the anus – are also between boys' and men's legs. Girls and women have these parts too.

The SCROTUM is a soft bag of squishy skin that holds the two testicles.

The PENIS hangs in front of the scrotum. Sometimes, penises get hard and stick out. That's called "having an erection". Baby boys, boys and men all have erections. Baby boys even have erections before they are born, while they are growing inside their mothers' bodies.

The small opening at the end of the penis – where pee comes out – is called the OPENING TO THE URETHRA.

Poo comes out of an opening called the ANUS.

Altogether, boys and men have two openings between their legs – the opening at the tip of the penis and the anus.

penis

opening to the urethra

scrotum

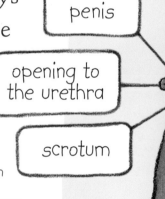

anus

bladder

urethra

vas deferens tubes

penis

testicle

testicle

The special parts INSIDE boys' and men's bodies are the two testicles and the two "vas deferens" tubes. Girls and women do not have these parts.

Two other parts – the bladder and the urethra – are also INSIDE boys' and men's bodies. Girls and women have these parts too.

A young *boy's* two TESTICLES are each about the size of a grape. Two small tubes – called the VAS DEFERENS – look like strands of cooked spaghetti.

Pee comes from the BLADDER and goes into a small tube inside the penis called the URETHRA. Pee leaves boys' and men's bodies through the small opening at the end of the penis.

The loose skin at the end of the penis is called the "foreskin". Some baby boys' foreskins are removed a few days after they are born. Some baby boys' foreskins are not removed. That's why some penises look different from other penises.

Penis with a foreskin
"uncircumcised" penis

Penis without a foreskin
"circumcised" penis

ALL birds and bees have wings!

What Girls Have

Baby girls are born with special parts of their bodies – outside and inside – that make them girls.

The special OUTSIDE parts – the vulva, the opening to the vagina and the clitoris – are between girls' and women's legs. That's why they are hard to see. Boys and men do not have these parts.

Two other OUTSIDE parts – the opening to the urethra and the anus – are also between girls' and women's legs. Boys and men have these parts too.

The VULVA is the area of soft skin between girls' and women's legs.

Inside the vulva is a small bump of skin, about the size of a pea, called the CLITORIS.

Also inside the vulva are two small openings – the OPENING TO THE URETHRA, where pee comes out – and the OPENING TO THE VAGINA.

Poo comes out of an opening called the ANUS.

Altogether, girls and women have three openings between their legs – the opening to the urethra, the opening to the vagina and the anus.

clitoris

opening to the urethra

opening to the vagina

vulva

anus

The special parts INSIDE girls' and women's bodies are the two ovaries, the two Fallopian tubes, the uterus and the vagina. Boys and men do not have these parts.

Two other parts – the bladder and the urethra – are also INSIDE girls' and women's bodies. Boys and men have these parts too.

A young girl's two OVARIES are each about the size of a grape.

The two FALLOPIAN TUBES are about as narrow as drinking straws.

The VAGINA is a stretchy tube that goes from the uterus to the outside of the body.

A young girl's UTERUS is about the size of a small plum.

Pee comes from the BLADDER and goes into a small tube called the URETHRA. Pee leaves girls' and women's bodies through the small opening at the end of the urethra.

Fallopian tubes

ovary

ovary

uterus

bladder

vagina

urethra

Knowing the names of ALL the parts of your body is—

PERFECTLY NORMAL!

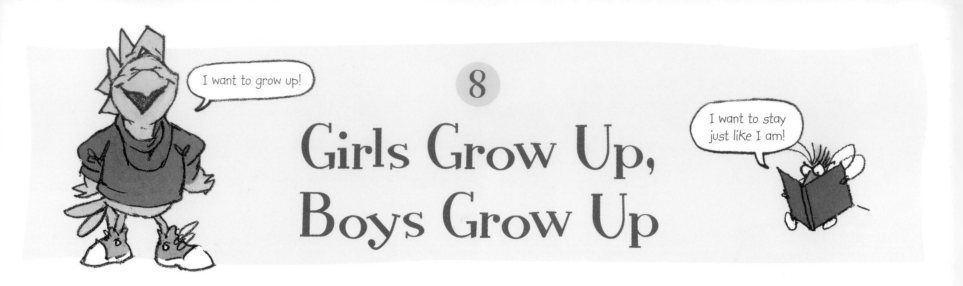

Girls Grow Up, Boys Grow Up

When boys and girls grow up, their bodies change and become grown-up bodies. That's when the special parts on the OUTSIDE and INSIDE of their bodies become parts that can help make a baby.

When a girl grows up, her body becomes a woman's body. That's when her breasts grow larger and hair grows under her arms and around her vulva. And that's when the ovaries begin to send out tiny eggs, also called "egg cells."

When a boy grows up, his body becomes a man's body. That's when hair grows on his face, under his arms, next to his penis and on his chest. That's when his voice begins to sound like a man's voice and his penis and scrotum grow larger. And that's when the testicles begin to make very, very tiny sperm, also called "sperm cells."

Wow! Kids grow up to be ... GROWN-UPS!

Well, du-uh! And boys grow up to be ... MEN! And girls grow up to be ... WOMEN!

So Many Eggs! So Many Sperm!

Just two things – one very tiny sperm from inside a man's body and one tiny egg from inside a woman's body – are needed to make a baby.

Every day, millions and millions of very, very tiny sperm are made in a man's testicles. Sperm are so tiny they can only be seen through a microscope.

Here's what sperm look like under a microscope.

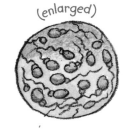

(enlarged)

Boys are born with testicles. But a boy's testicles CANNOT make sperm until his body has become a man's body. That is why boys' bodies cannot help make a baby.

Sperm? Like a sperm whale?

I don't think so! Sperm are tiny! Whales are huge!

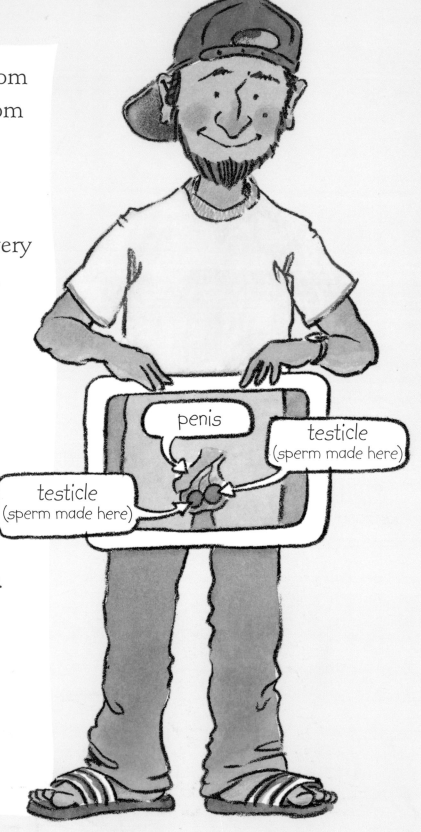

penis

testicle (sperm made here)

testicle (sperm made here)

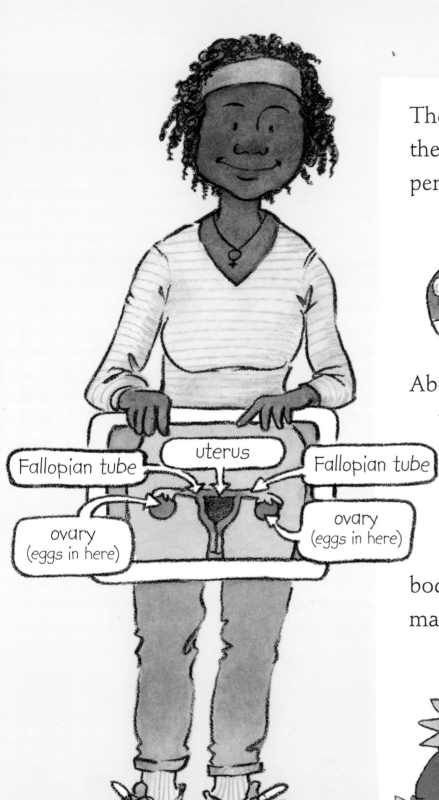

ovary
(eggs in here)

Fallopian tube

uterus

Fallopian tube

ovary
(eggs in here)

There are thousands of very tiny eggs in the ovaries. Each egg is about the size of a pencil dot.

(enlarged)

Here's what eggs look like under a microscope.

About once a month, an egg pops out of a woman's ovary and into one of her two Fallopian tubes. Girls are born with eggs in their ovaries. But a girl's eggs ARE NOT READY to help make a baby until her body has become a woman's body. That is why girls' bodies cannot make a baby.

Eggs? Like the kind you eat with bacon or sausage??

I don't think so! Those are chickens' eggs — not humans' eggs!

10
Making a Baby

To make a baby, a sperm from a man's body and an egg from a woman's body must get together.

1 sperm   1 egg   1 baby

When grown-ups want to make a baby, most often a woman and a man have a special kind of loving called "making love", "having sex" or "sex". This kind of loving happens when the woman and the man get so close to each other that the man's penis goes inside the woman's vagina.

Children are much too young to do the special kind of loving – called "sex" – that grown-ups do.

When grown-ups have sex, sperm can swim out through the small opening at the tip of the man's penis – and into the woman's vagina. Then the sperm swim through her vagina, through her uterus and into her two Fallopian tubes.

If just one sperm meets and joins together with an egg that's in one of the Fallopian tubes – an amazing thing can happen! The beginning cells of a baby can start to grow!

Sometimes a sperm and egg are not able to meet inside a woman's body. That's when a doctor can take an egg and a sperm and put them into a little dish where the sperm can swim into the egg. Then the doctor puts the egg inside the woman's uterus and the beginning cells of a baby can start to grow. Or the doctor can put sperm into the woman's vagina, where the sperm swim until they meet an egg in one of her Fallopian tubes.

The BIG Swim

31

The Growing Womb

Oh, so the growing baby grows in THE GROWING WOMB! Get it?

The uterus is also called "the womb". Once the ball of cells plants itself in the womb, that's when a woman is "pregnant". "Pregnant" means the woman is going to have a baby. The woman is pregnant until her baby is born. It's hard to believe that a tiny ball of cells can grow into a whole new person – a baby! But it can.

Well, it sure doesn't grow in THE LIVING WOMB! Got it!

Pinpoint to Watermelon

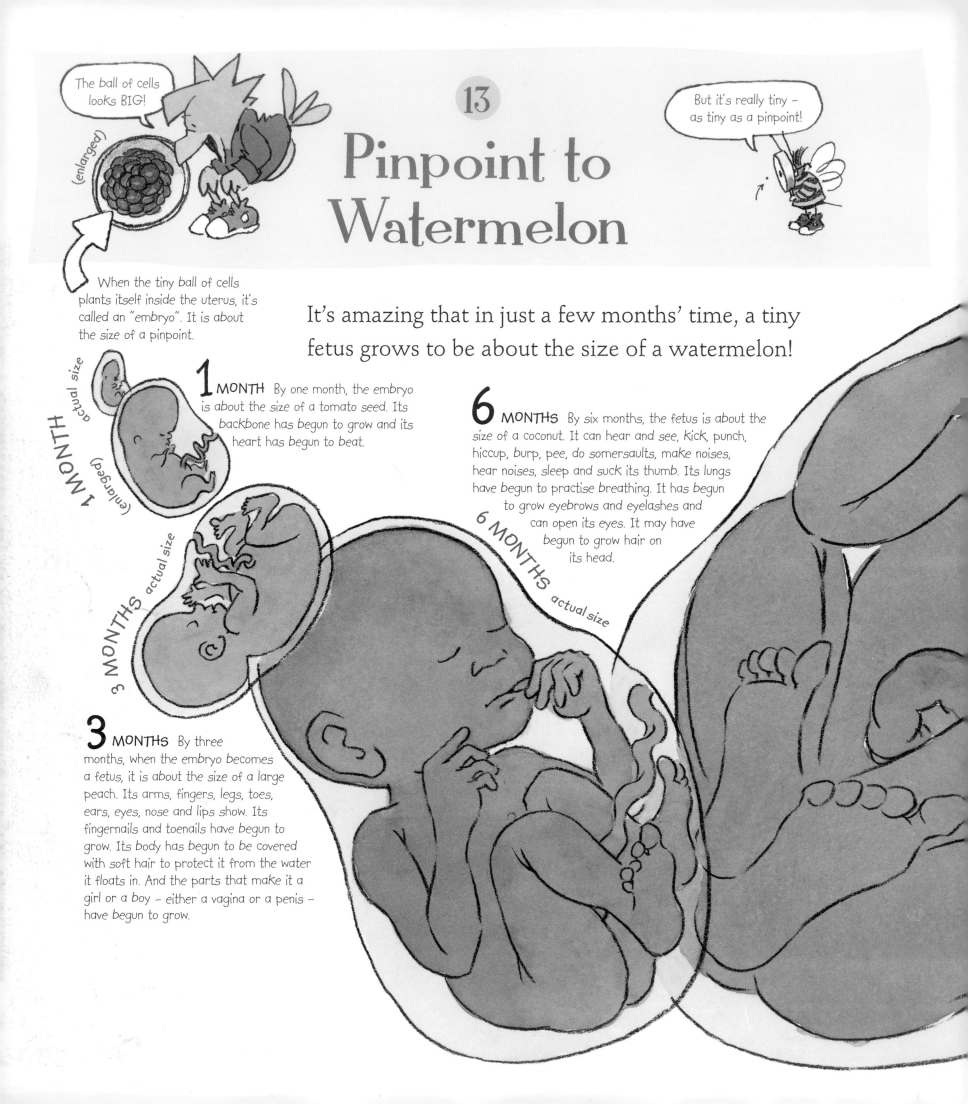

The ball of cells looks BIG!

(enlarged)

But it's really tiny – as tiny as a pinpoint!

When the tiny ball of cells plants itself inside the uterus, it's called an "embryo". It is about the size of a pinpoint.

It's amazing that in just a few months' time, a tiny fetus grows to be about the size of a watermelon!

1 MONTH By one month, the embryo is about the size of a tomato seed. Its backbone has begun to grow and its heart has begun to beat.

1 MONTH actual size

(enlarged)

6 MONTHS By six months, the fetus is about the size of a coconut. It can hear and see, kick, punch, hiccup, burp, pee, do somersaults, make noises, hear noises, sleep and suck its thumb. Its lungs have begun to practise breathing. It has begun to grow eyebrows and eyelashes and can open its eyes. It may have begun to grow hair on its head.

3 MONTHS actual size

6 MONTHS actual size

3 MONTHS By three months, when the embryo becomes a fetus, it is about the size of a large peach. Its arms, fingers, legs, toes, ears, eyes, nose and lips show. Its fingernails and toenails have begun to grow. Its body has begun to be covered with soft hair to protect it from the water it floats in. And the parts that make it a girl or a boy – either a vagina or a penis – have begun to grow.

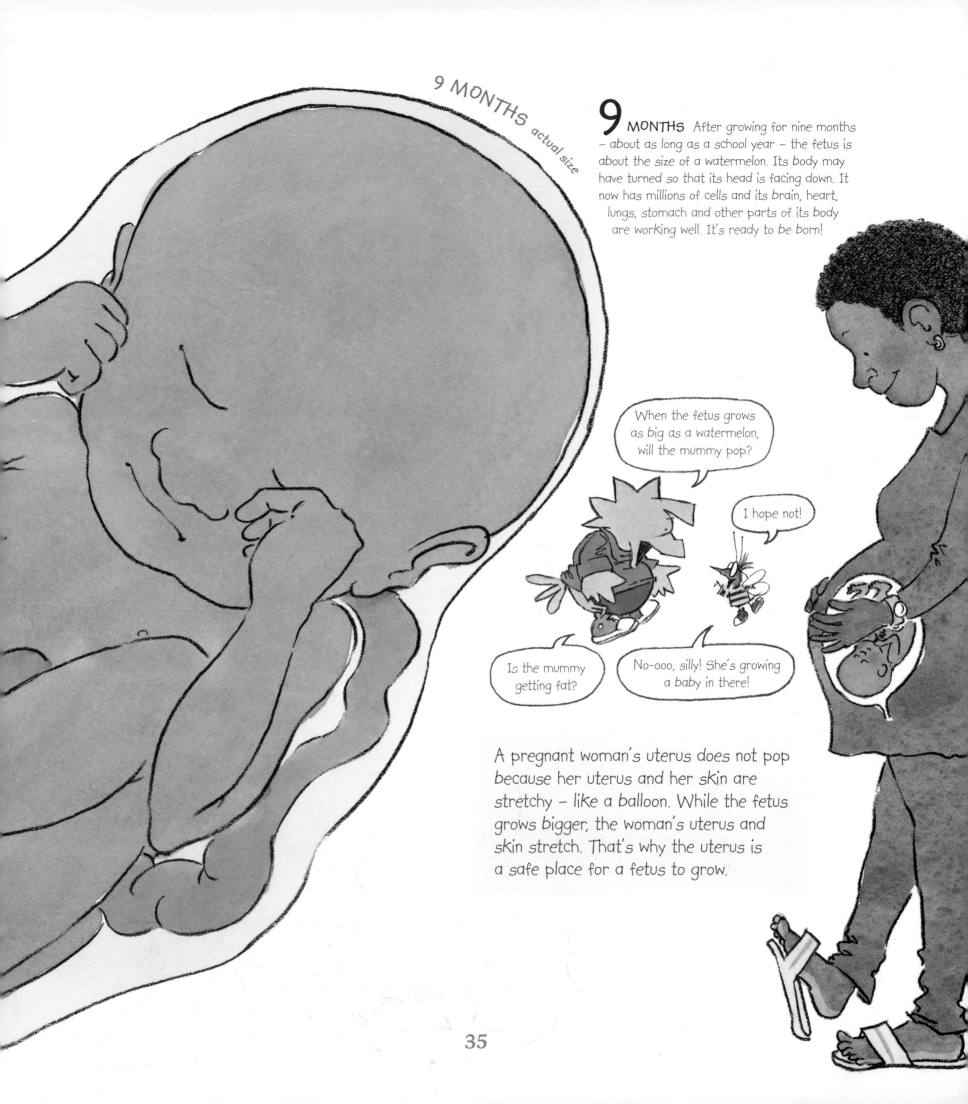

9 MONTHS
After growing for nine months – about as long as a school year – the fetus is about the size of a watermelon. Its body may have turned so that its head is facing down. It now has millions of cells and its brain, heart, lungs, stomach and other parts of its body are working well. It's ready to be born!

When the fetus grows as big as a watermelon, will the mummy pop?

I hope not!

Is the mummy getting fat?

No-ooo, silly! She's growing a baby in there!

A pregnant woman's uterus does not pop *because* her uterus and her *skin* are stretchy – like a balloon. While the fetus grows bigger, the woman's uterus and skin stretch. That's why the uterus is a safe place for a fetus to grow.

The Twisty Cord

We have to eat to grow. I have to eat 'cos I'm a growing bird!

I'll have honey on toast, please.

A fetus gets the good things it needs to grow and stay healthy from the food a pregnant woman eats and drinks – and from the fresh air she breathes.

The oxygen in the air and bits of food and drink travel from the pregnant woman's body to the fetus through a twisty cord that's attached to the fetus's body. This is the umbilical cord. Your tummy button is the place where the cord was attached to you when you were growing inside the uterus. "Navel" is another word for tummy button.

Are you an "outie" or an "innie"?

I don't know. I've never checked to see if my tummy button sticks in or out.

The uterus is filled with warm water. That's what keeps the fetus warm and protects it from bumps and pokes. Sometimes the fetus drinks the water it floats in and pees a little bit. The fetus's pee leaves a pregnant woman's body with her pee. Most fetuses do not poo inside the uterus.

Phew! So glad the fetus doesn't poo in there.

Sounds nice in there. Like being in a fishbowl, but with warm water and soft sides. Must be fun – floating in the uterus.

HOW A FETUS EATS AND BREATHES

1 Fresh air goes into the woman's nose and mouth.

2 Food – like a banana – and drinks – like milk – go into her mouth.

3 Air goes into the woman's two lungs.

4 Food and drinks go through the woman's stomach.

5 Inside her stomach, the food breaks into tiny bits.

6 The bits of food and air travel into the fetus's body through the twisty cord.

brain thinking of baby names

Robie Mary Lee
Ella Daisy
Rosie Bill
Sam
Michael

pregnant woman

lung

lung

stomach

uterus

fetus

lunch

Oh, so-ooo the twisty cord's like a straw. Food and drinks and air come into the twisty cord – and go right to the fetus.

And you don't even need a spoon or fork to eat like that!

pregnant dog

puppy fetuses

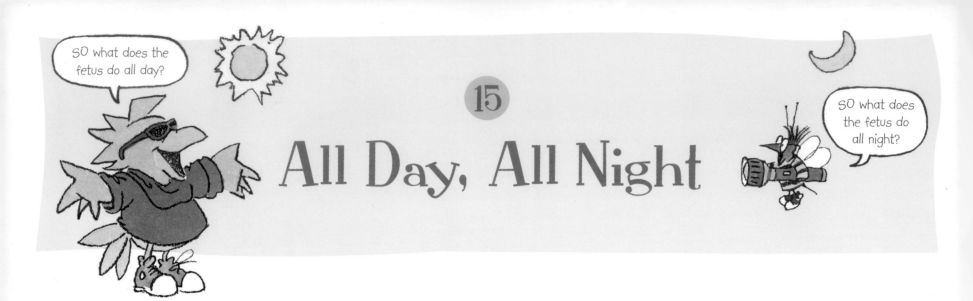

All Day, All Night

While the fetus is growing inside the uterus, it can do so many things! It can kick and punch, do somersaults, suck its thumb and fingers, taste, swallow, blink, stretch, sleep and make noises – like hiccups and burps.

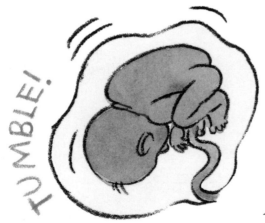

As the fetus grows bigger, it can hear the sound of voices and other noises too – like a doorbell ringing or someone singing. It can hear its mother's heart beating and her stomach grumbling, and it can see bright light.

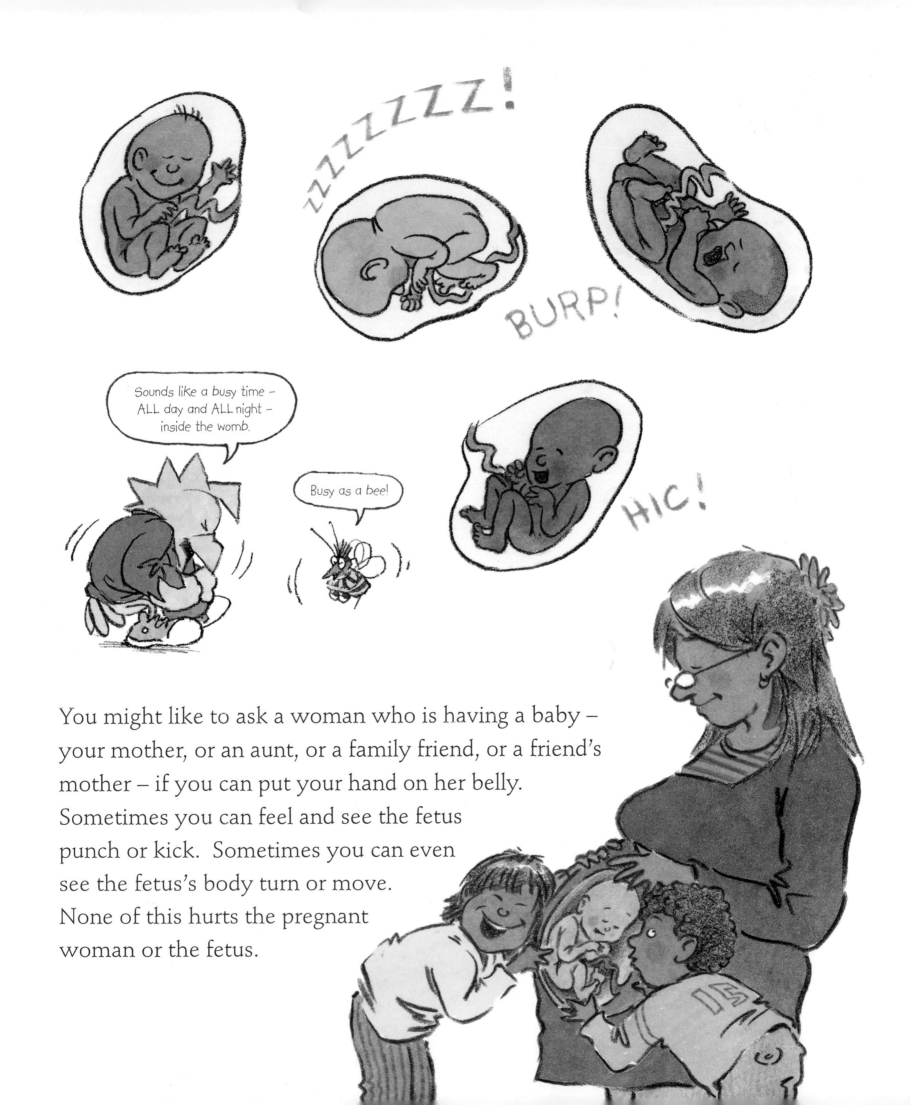

You might like to ask a woman who is having a baby – your mother, or an aunt, or a family friend, or a friend's mother – if you can put your hand on her belly. Sometimes you can feel and see the fetus punch or kick. Sometimes you can even see the fetus's body turn or move. None of this hurts the pregnant woman or the fetus.

Boy? Girl? 1 Baby? 2 or More?

How do you know if the baby is going to be a boy or a girl or—

one baby or more?

When a doctor or nurse takes a moving computer picture of the fetus inside the uterus – called an "ultrasound" – sometimes you can see the fetus moving, punching, kicking or sleeping. Sometimes you can see if the fetus has a penis. If it does, it will be born a boy. If it doesn't, it has a vulva and will be born a girl. That's how some families know before their baby is born whether it will be a boy or a girl.

Some families choose not to look and find out if their baby will be born a girl or a boy. They want to be surprised. They wait until the baby is born to find out. Some families bring home a computer picture of the fetus to show to the rest of their family and their friends.

When a doctor or nurse takes a computer picture, they can also find out if a pregnant woman has one, two or even more fetuses growing inside her uterus.

COMPUTER PICTURE OF A FETUS

Wow! A computer can see inside my body!

I don't want to see inside ANYBODY!

Usually only one fetus is growing in the uterus.
Sometimes there are two, three or more.

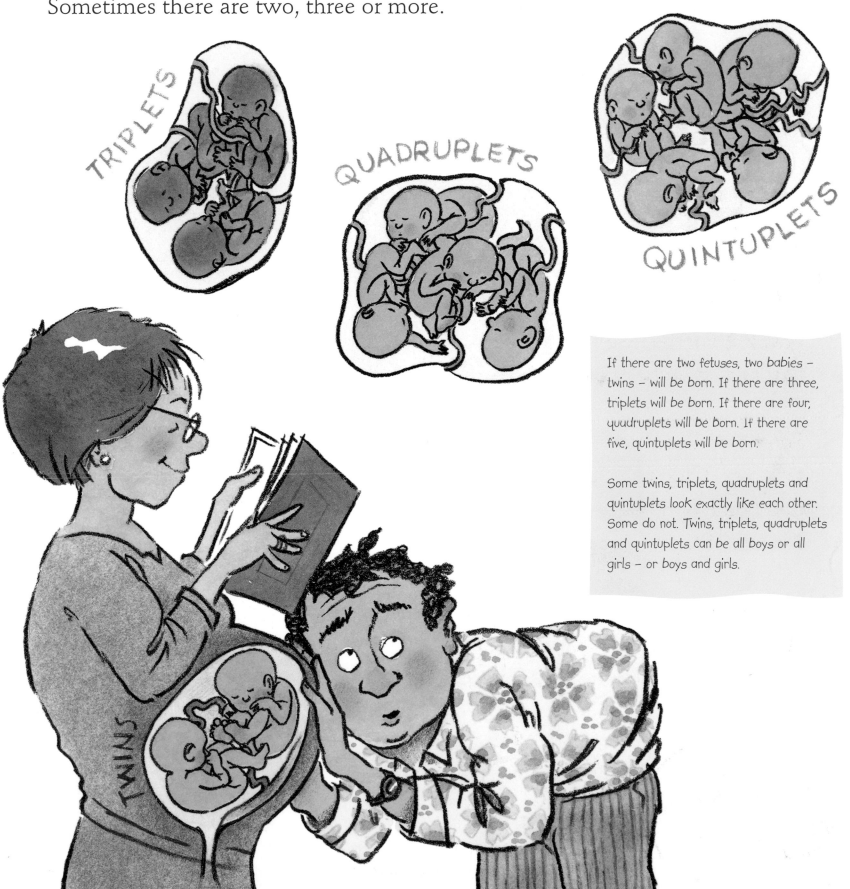

If there are two fetuses, two babies –
twins – will be born. If there are three,
triplets will be born. If there are four,
quadruplets will be born. If there are
five, quintuplets will be born.

Some twins, triplets, quadruplets and
quintuplets look exactly like each other.
Some do not. Twins, triplets, quadruplets
and quintuplets can be all boys or all
girls – or boys and girls.

It's a Baby!

Most babies are born in a hospital. Some babies are born at home. Almost always, special people – doctors or midwives, nurses or doulas – help the mummy while her baby is being born. Often the daddy or the partner, or sometimes aunts, uncles, grandparents or good friends, also help.

When a baby is ready to be born, the muscles inside the mummy's uterus push the baby out of the uterus and through the mummy's vagina. The vagina stretches to make room for the baby as it slides out – and is born! Most babies are born this way.

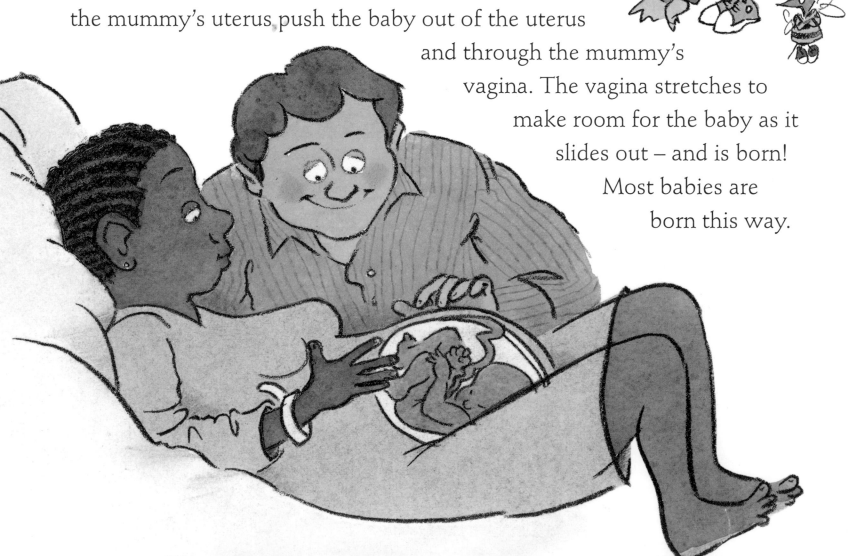

Another way a baby is born is when the doctor makes a cut through the mummy's skin and into her uterus. The mummy is given a special medicine before the cutting so that it won't hurt. After the cutting, the baby is lifted out of the uterus – and is born! Then the cut is sewn up with special thread. Many babies are born this way. This kind of birth is called a "cesarean birth" or a "c-section".

You might like to ask your parent which way you were born and if you were born at a hospital or at home.

I pecked my way out of my eggshell. That's how I was born.

When I was born – I hatched out of my egg.

The moment a baby is born, someone usually shouts out, "IT'S A GIRL!" or "IT'S A BOY!" – even if the parent or parents already knew the baby would be a girl or boy. The moment a baby is born is so exciting!

It's a BABY!

Happy Birthday!

Most babies let out a cry the moment they are born. That's how a baby begins to breathe on his or her own. As soon as the baby is born, the twisty cord that attached the growing baby to its mummy is cut. The cutting does not hurt the baby or the mummy.

The cord is cut because now the baby can breathe air on its own. And now the new baby can drink with its mouth from its mummy's breasts or from a bottle. Milk from the mummy's breasts or special milk from a bottle is all the food a new baby needs.

My family was so happy to see me and cuddle me and call me "Sweetie Birdy"!

The place where the cord was attached becomes the baby's tummy button. As soon as the cord is cut – and sometimes even before – the baby's parent or parents can hold and cuddle and kiss the new baby at last. It feels so wonderful to hold and look at the new baby!

My family was so happy to see me and cuddle me and call me "Honeybunch"!

The day you were born was your "birth day" and that never changes. The word "birth" means "the beginning of something new" or "a new baby". Each year on your birthday, everyone loves to sing "Happy Birthday!" to you because they are so excited and happy that you were born.

19
Cuddles and Kisses

All babies do is cry, sleep, pee, poo – and take baths too.

That's OK. Kids and grown-ups do these things too.

Most kids and grown-ups can't remember being a baby. You might want to ask your parent or parents to show you pictures of yourself when you were little. Or you could ask them to tell you stories about all the amazing things you could do and what you were like when you were little.

If you watch a new baby, you'll see that new babies can do lots of things. They often get tired because they are doing so many new things. That's why they sleep a lot – and cry a lot.

Babies cry when they are tired or hungry. They also cry when they have peed or pooed and need a dry nappy.

When babies are hungry, they can suck and drink special milk from their mummy's breasts or from a bottle. Babies cry when they need a cuddle and kiss or when they are too hot or too cold. Crying is one of the ways babies tell us what they want and how they feel.

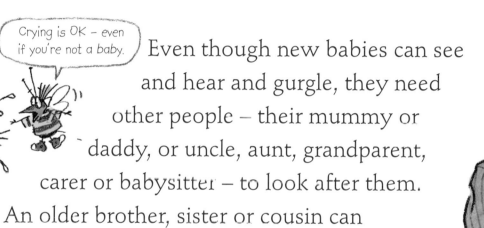

"Babies are crybabies."

"Crying is OK – even if you're not a baby."

Even though new babies can see and hear and gurgle, they need other people – their mummy or daddy, or uncle, aunt, grandparent, carer or babysitter – to look after them. An older brother, sister or cousin can help change a nappy, help give a bath and when babies are older – help feed them. They can also play games with the baby – like "Peekaboo! I Love You!"

Babies also love to be cuddled, kissed, smiled at, talked to and sung to by older sisters and brothers and cousins. Babies love to be with older kids!

47

All Kinds of Families

I have a very nice family!

I have a very sweet family!

Almost all babies grow up in and are loved and taken care of by a family. Most babies are born into their family. Some babies and children are adopted into their family.

Some families have one child. Some families have two, or three, or four or more children. Some families have a mummy and a daddy. Some have a mummy. Some have a daddy. Some have two mummies. Some have two daddies. Some kids live with a parent and step-parent, or with an aunt, an uncle, a grandmother or grandfather, or with a foster parent. Some kids live with one parent part of the time and with their other parent the rest of the time.

Sometimes, a parent – or parents – cannot take care of their baby or child. So they make a plan for their baby or child to be adopted – to become part of another family. And that baby or child lives with, grows up with and is loved and taken care of by the parent or parents who adopt them. And the baby or child becomes part of that parent's or parents' family. When that happens, it's called "adoption".

Parents, sisters, brothers, cousins, aunts, uncles and grandparents are all part of a person's family. And for many people, good friends, babysitters and nannies are part of their families too.

OK Touches, Not-OK Touches

Babies, kids, teenagers and grown-ups all need cuddles and hugs and kisses from the people who are good to us and love us. The everyday hugs and kisses and touching and holding hands with our families and good friends are "OK touches". There are "OK touches" and "NOT-OK touches".

The parts of our bodies that are under our pants or swimsuits are called our "private parts". If you touch or rub the private parts of your own body because it tickles and feels good, that's an "OK touch".

Well, my "private parts" are under my feathers.

Well, my whole body is private – and that's THAT!

During a check-up, the reason your doctor or nurse has to look at and touch your "private parts" is to make sure that every part of your body is healthy. This kind of touching done by a doctor or nurse is also an "OK touch".

STOP! NO! DON'T!

If anyone touches your "private parts" – or any other part of your body that you do not want them to touch – these are all "not-OK touches". If this happens to you, tell that person "STOP!" or "NO!" or "DON'T!" – even if the person is someone in your family, or a friend, or someone you know or you love – or is bigger, older or stronger than you are.

I'm very small, you know.

But big enough to say "NO!", "STOP!" or "DON'T!"

If any kind of "not-OK touch" happens to you, tell a grown-up right away – even if the person who touched you tells you to keep it a secret. This is a secret you have to tell someone.

Tell someone in your family, or your teacher, doctor or nurse, or your school nurse or someone you know very well. If the first person you tell does not help you or believe you, keep on telling people until someone believes you. That person will do everything she or he can to help keep you safe and protect you and to make the "not-OK touches" stop. Luckily there are many grown-ups who can and will help.

Talking about this is scary...

Talking about this makes me feel better... Need a hug?

I do ... my friend.

Here's a NOT-too-tight hug, my friend.

Girls, Boys, Friends

As you grow up from a baby to a little kid to a big kid – it's fun to have a friend. It doesn't matter how many friends you have, or if your friends are boys, or girls or girls and boys. What matters most is being a good friend.

Taking turns, sharing a toy or playing a game together are great ways to be a good friend. Being nice when a friend feels bad or sad or angry is another way to be a good friend.

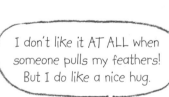

Saying "I'm sorry!" is also a way to be a good friend. So is holding hands, giving a hug or just talking to a friend.

SO-OOO what's a girlfriend – and a boyfriend?

That's when teenagers get all smoochy and lovey-dovey. Some grown-ups have girlfriends and boyfriends too. But we just have friends.

Any time you do not want to hold hands, or be touched, or hugged or kissed by a friend – it's OK to tell a friend that. Or if a friend does not want to hold hands, or be touched, or hugged or kissed by you, that's OK too. Good friends listen to each other.

I don't want to do THAT!

OK.

If a friend asks you to do something you don't want to do or think you shouldn't do – like climbing too high, or teasing someone or taking off your clothes – you can say, "No, I won't do that!" or "I don't want to do that" – even if your friends tell you it's OK to do it.

You don't have to do everything a friend tells or asks you to do. Friends do not have to do everything you tell them to do. It's also OK for friends to do different things – and even get cross with each other. No matter what, it's so good to have a friend.

Glad you are my friend, my friend.

Phew! Glad to hear that, my friend.

53

Growing Up

I can't wait to be a grown-up!

I like me just the way I am – NOT grown-up – NOT yet!

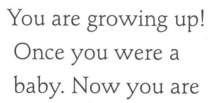

You are growing up! Once you were a baby. Now you are a kid. One day you will be a teenager. It's hard to believe, but some day you will be a grown-up. You might even decide to be a mummy or a daddy. And when you are even older, you may become a grandpa or a grandma!

Growing up

Girls grow up to be women. Boys grow up to be men. Growing up takes a long time and a lot of years.

is so amazing!

Bee-lieve It!

Thank You!

TINA ALU, family planning director, Cambridge Economic Opportunity Committee, Cambridge, Massachusetts

BETSY ANDERSON, Kindergarten teacher, Shady Hill School, Cambridge, Massachusetts

SARAH BIRSS, M.D., pediatrician/child psychiatrist, Cambridge, Massachusetts

DEBORAH CHAMBERLAIN, research associate, Norwood, Massachusetts

NANCY CLOSE, PH.D., assistant professor, Yale University Child Study Center, New Haven, Connecticut

SALLY CRISSMAN, science educator, Watertown, Massachusetts

MARY DOMINGUEZ, elementary science educator, Belmont Public Schools, Belmont, Massachusetts

BEN H. HARRIS, parent, New York, New York

BILL HARRIS, grandparent, Cambridge, Massachusetts

DAVID B. HARRIS, parent, New York, New York

EMILY B. HARRIS, parent, New York, New York

HILARY G. HARRIS, parent, New York, New York

ROBYN HEILBRUN, grandparent, Salt Lake City, Utah

CARLA HORWITZ, ED.D., director, Calvin Hill Day Care Center; Kindergarten lecturer, Yale University Child Study Center and Department of Psychology, New Haven, Connecticut

LESLIE KANTOR, M.P.H., director of education, Planned Parenthood of New York City, New York, New York

JILL KANTROWITZ, director of education, Planned Parenthood League of Massachusetts, Boston, Massachusetts

MARGOT KAPLAN-SANOFF, ED.D., infant and child development specialist, Head Start Training and Technical Assistance Quality Initiative, Boston, Massachusetts

ELLEN KELLEY, early childhood consultant, Arlington, Massachusetts

SALLY LESSER, bookseller, Cambridge, Massachusetts

AMY LEVINE, family project coordinator, Sexuality Information and Education Council of the United States, New York, New York

ELIZABETH A. LEVY, children's book author, New York, New York

ALICIA F. LIEBERMAN, PH.D., professor of medical psychology, University of California at San Francisco, San Francisco, California

CAROL LYNCH, M.ED., sexuality educator, Arlington, Massachusetts

STEVEN MARANS, PH.D., professor of child psychiatry and psychiatry, Yale University Child Study Center, New Haven, Connecticut

WENDY DALTON MARANS, M.SC., associate research scientist, Yale University Child Study Center, New Haven, Connecticut

LINDA C. MAYES, M.D., Arnold Gesell professor of child psychiatry, pediatrics, and psychology, Yale University Child Study Center, New Haven, Connecticut; co-chairman of directorial team, Anna Freud Centre, London, UK

MICHAEL McGEE, vice president for education, Planned Parenthood Federation of America, New York, New York

ELI NEWBERGER, M.D., senior associate in medicine, Children's Hospital; assistant professor of pediatrics, Harvard Medical School, Boston, Massachusetts

JANET PATTERSON, M.ED., librarian, Advent School, Boston, Massachusetts

LAURA RILEY, M.D., obstetrician/gynecologist, director, OB/GYN Infectious Diseases, Massachusetts General Hospital, Boston, Massachusetts

MONICA RODRIQUEZ, vice president for education and training, Sexuality Information and Education Council of the United States, New York, New York

HEATHER Z. SANKEY, M.D., obstetrician/gynecologist, residency program director, Baystate Medical Center, Springfield, Massachusetts

KAREN SHORR, M.A.T., preKindergarten teacher, The Brookwood School, Manchester, Massachusetts

VICTORIA SOLOMON, children's librarian, Cambridge Public Library, Cambridge, Massachusetts

SUSAN WEBBER, consultant, Arlington, Massachusetts

ELAINE WINTER, M.ED., lower school principal, Little Red School House, New York, New York

MARY YOUNG, M.ED., assistant director of early childhood admissions, early childhood learning specialist, Little Red School House, New York, New York

PAMELA M. ZUCKERMAN, M.D., pediatrician, Brookline, Massachusetts

And a giant thanks to everyone at Candlewick Press, especially to MARY LEE DONOVAN and CAROLINE LAWRENCE for understanding and supporting our vision, to ANDREA TOMPA for keeping track of everything, and to EMIL FORTUNE and LUCY INGRAMS at Walker Books UK for making sure our books work for children and families across the big pond.

Here's a list of all the things in this book – all the things you might want to find out about!

The **BOLD** numbers are the page numbers WHERE you can find out what a word means.

Index

First published 2006 by Walker Books Ltd
87 Vauxhall Walk, London SE11 5HJ

This edition published 2007

2 4 6 8 10 9 7 5 3 1

Text © 2006 BEE Productions, Inc.
Illustrations © 2006 BIRD Productions, Inc.

The right of Robie H. Harris and Michael Emberley to be identified as author and illustrator respectively
of this work has been asserted by them in accordance with the Copyright, Designs and Patents Act 1988

This book has been typeset in StempelSchneidler

Printed in China

British Library Cataloguing in Publication Data:
a catalogue record for this book
is available from the British Library

ISBN 978-1-4063-0606-4

www.walkerbooks.co.uk

Every Human Child Wonders...

"*Let's Talk* gives children the gentle truth about being born and growing up. Even the youngest children notice, wonder and need to know who they are, where they came from, how they got here and what makes them the same or not the same as their friends. Every human child wonders these things but not all of them ask, and not all their parents know just what to tell and when and how. This delightful book is an essential family resource full of accurate, comforting and positive information. Parents can read the book to children, bit by bit, and then keep it around – so they can look at the pictures and one day, read it by themselves."

Penelope Leach, Ph.D., author of Your Baby & Child *and* Children First

All this stuff about bodies and babies is – AMAZING!

So, ENOUGH about all that stuff – for now!